(quiet, space).

a place for rest, reflection, and creation.

Erin Schalk

Bridging Art

www.erinschalk.com | www.bridgingart.com

P.O. Box 2101
Anaheim, CA 92814

Ordering Information:

Quantity sales. Discounts are available on quantity purchases by corporations, associations, and others. For details, contact the "Special Sales Department" at the address above.

(quiet, space). a place for rest, reflection, and creation / Erin Schalk.
– 1st ed.

ISBN: 978-0-578-31110-4

www.ingramcontent.com/pod-product-compliance
Lightning Source LLC
Chambersburg PA
CBHW061006050726
47592CB00003B/1364
9780976158394

I will record a small portion of today because I am a living, breathing, sentient being who had the privilege of getting up and experiencing this day. Thank you for the gift.

And, here is my gift in return.

(ii)

story.

Dear reader, my story may be like your story. Or, the story of someone you know. We are living in challenging times where there is often far too much pressure placed upon us, continually propelling us to do more and be more – sometimes, to the point of complete burnout. Our attention is often distracted, fragmented, and lacking a clear focus. Not only are we expected to do so much but also feel compelled to complete everything at the speed of light, leaving us feeling thoroughly scattered and depleted at the end of the day.

Even in rare moments of rest, solitude, or unstructured time, we may be unable to reap the benefits. We may find ourselves stopping our quiet thoughts to reflexively check our phone, texts, and multiple email accounts.

More troubling still, our true, authentic connections to others such as family and friends, as well as our connection to ourselves, can become like frayed threads. Left untended for too long, these threads become so worn that they can snap apart. In the aftermath, we may find entire sections of our lives completely unraveling.

If you consider yourself a creative person and an artist in your own right, overwork, unrealistic and unsustainable productivity, chronic stress, and lack of proper self-care take on additional dimensions and dangers. Over time, you may find your desire to innovate and experiment with new ideas, as well as your creative work itself, quietly eroding away.

Even if you do not consider yourself creative in a traditional sense such as an artist, poet, musician, dancer, actor, or similar, know that each human being has a unique manifestation of creativity. Your creativity may be a gift for leadership, car repair, designing and cultivating an aromatic herb garden, and more. Whatever your situation, know that you – as a beautiful human being – can benefit from taking time to allow your body and mind to rest on these pages.

(iii)

collaboration.

With **(quiet, space).**, I invite you into a collaboration. By pausing to reflect and respond to the prompts in this book, you have my full permission (**see if you can grant yourself the permission as well*) to use this space as a resting place to soften your thoughts and make more room in your life for daydreaming.

At the same time, consider this book to be your personal launching pad. When you are rested and ready, take the thoughts, responses, and ideas you generate from these exercises and use them as fuel for future projects that (1) bring you joy and (2) allow you to more fully share your unique gifts with the wider world.

May this book assist you in some small (*or perhaps large*) ways with appreciating the greater beauty in life that is for each of us. May you find rest, as well as reignite the passion and creativity that you feel you have (*temporarily, please trust me*) lost.

Most sincerely,
Erin

(iv)

disclaimer.

This book periodically discusses general health information, self-care, mental health, and similar subjects. As a reminder, content from this journal, including regular journaling, writing, and creative practices, are not substitutes for medical, psychological, emotional, and/or mental health treatments from qualified healthcare professionals. If you have a medical, psychological, emotional, and/or mental health concern, you should seek consultation, advice, and treatment from your professional health care provider(s) immediately. If you are considering harming yourself, please go to **crisistextline.org** to speak with a volunteer counselor.

(v)

guidelines for using this book.

There are infinite ways to approach working through this book. Consider everything listed below as mere suggestions and nothing more. If you are not sure where to begin, use the ideas below as footholds to help you get started. Improvisation and shattering the rules are more than welcome. Circle or highlight the ideas that are most helpful for you, and use the blank space on the next pages to map out additional thoughts.

- If you are struggling with pressure to be productive in all areas of your life, resist the temptation to assign yourself quotas *(such as, "I will complete ___ number of pages in ___ days")*. You can complete this book in a few weeks, months, or take even longer. Pace yourself.

- Allow yourself to work in a nonlinear fashion. Select a prompt that is most interesting to you on that particular day, in that particular moment.

- If possible, keep an additional journal, notebook, or sketchbook nearby in case you require more space to record all of your thoughts.

- As best as possible, allow yourself to work through this book during moments of quiet.

- Depending on your situation (*for example, if you have small children*), solitude and silence may be difficult to come by. Long stretches of time for reflection are wonderful but may be an out-of-reach luxury in this stage of your life. Consider writing for five minute intervals and work your way up to longer stretches, if possible.

- Within these pages, allow yourself the freedom to experiment. If you are a writer, you may be tempted to write all of your responses to the prompts. Gently stretch yourself. You can try paper collage, drawing with markers, abstract mark-making, and similar.

- Resist the urge to edit or curate. Allow your responses, whenever possible, to be immediate, diverse, and authentic. Think stream of consciousness.

If you'd like, use this space to list your own guidelines:

part one:
poetry fragments
(i - xv).

guidelines for poetry fragments.

Over the course of the following pages, you will find a series of short-verse poems and poetry fragments. Allow yourself time to pause and linger over the words, as well as any images, memories, or sensations they bring to mind.

Once you feel ready, use these clusters of words as inspiration for your own reflections. Brief questions are also provided for each fragment, if you need a little help to get started, or if you find yourself worn down in body and mind and ideas are not *(yet)* moving.

Feel free to try any of the suggested ideas listed below. Better still, experiment with your own unique approaches.

- Journal about your personal reflections on the poetry fragment. Regard the piece as a mini-retreat where you have the freedom to write and explore any and all individual responses.

- Consider the poem a starting point or prompt. Finish the piece, writing your own lines and verses however you like. You may end up with an entirely new poem or even song lyrics.

- While allowing the poetry fragment to soak in, notice any ideas or memories that immediately spring to mind. Select a memory that is especially vivid, and let this be a starting point for your own poem, prose piece, or private journal reflection.

- Select one of the words or a phrase from the fragment. Set a timer for five minutes and speed write *(i.e. write without stopping and avoid editing what comes forth)* on everything you can think of related to that word.

For example, if the word is "gold," you might find yourself writing about the gold ring your mother gave you as a graduation present, the last time you saw a golden moon, or the way the color gold gives you a feeling of warmth.

- Experiment with rearranging the word order in the fragment. Try weaving in new words. See how the meanings and moods conveyed by words can shift dramatically with just a few small changes.

- Working with someone you trust, pass this book back and forth, allowing each person to add their responses and ideas. Think of this as writing as conversation.

- If you do not feel compelled to write at the moment, respond to or build upon the fragment by different creative means such as dance, paper collage, clay, or similar.

If you'd like, use the space below to list your own ideas and methods:

(i)

vast mountain range splits
the horizon, spilled ink sky
fades to blue, then gold

[optional starting point:
what type(s) of landscapes or settings allow me to feel the most at peace?]

(i) **my response:**

(ii)

mountains feathered mist
evaporates into void
above still waters

[optional starting point:
what are some ways I can cultivate empty spaces in my life?
how do I define empty or emptiness?]

(ii) **my response:**

(iii)

faded mountain peak
crowned with evening's last cloud
...a complete stillness

[<u>optional starting point:</u>
am I currently experiencing a transition of any kind?
how can I navigate this liminal, in-between sort of space?]

(iii) **my response:**

(iv)

it had been sixteen years
since I last experienced the dawn
of an Iowa frost –

the clouds were fish vertebrae, fading
into an unbroken sky
of soft sterling...

[<u>optional starting point:</u>
what is a person, place, or experience I long for and why?
if the why is unclear now, what are some possible reasons?]

(iv) **my response:**

(v)

an evening snowfall
I lift my face to heaven
flakes are falling stars

[optional starting point:
pause and notice.
what sensations am I experiencing in my physical body at this moment?]

(v) **my response:**

(vi)

Texas springtime rains –
the waterfall of droplets
ring sonorously

[optional starting point:
pause and notice.
what sounds am I hearing at this moment?
if sound is not accessible to me, what movements, textures, or
vibrations am I feeling?]

(vi) **my response:**

(vii)

rain-soaked hibiscus
petals bow, a scalloped skirt
hem stroking the ground

[optional starting point:
what seemingly two dissimilar things can I compare or synthesize?
can I find overlap in aspects of my life where there seems, on the surface, to be none?]

(vii) **my response:**

(viii)

blanket of palm fronds
swaying beyond the window
dance of summer wind

[optional starting point:
consider season-to-season transitions such as autumn to winter or winter to spring.
what do I associate with each seasonal change?]

(viii) **my response:**

(ix)

scattered coral, a prism of
iced lavender and flickering gold,
guarded by wild orange clownfish

I can't help but wonder...

if life below the water's surface
is also enjoying
the spectacle above

[optional starting point:
what are my first thoughts on surfaces, submerging, floating,
looking up, or looking down?]

(ix) **my response:**

(x)

tense strokes land and lift
painting a plum hummingbird
in effortless flight

[<u>optional starting point:</u>
what contrasts are present in my life at this time?
example: a person who exudes calm in day-to-day interactions
may struggle internally with anxiety.]

(x) **my response:**

(xi)

delayed flight

spring rains stop; birds sing outside the window
a young sparrow lands on a brick wall;
the border that stitches together
the neighborhood's backyards.

she slips under the wall's ledge,
and an unexpected roof shelters her head
searching for her stolen sky, she cranes
her neck upward but is trapped under
the ledge's heavy ceiling, lost
under its blanketed shadow

wingtips graze brick, her
beak slides beyond the ledge, rush
of cyan freedom

[optional starting point:
in what ways have I recently felt tethered or caged?
despite this, how can I breathe and expand beyond these constrictions?]

(xi) **my response:**

(xii)

surrender to loss
when striving to cling tightly —
this immense courage

[optional starting point:
what have I let go?
what can I still let go?
what does radical letting go look like to me?]

(xii) **my response:**

(xiii)

sheltering in place
daily walk to the mailbox
warm sun, faded skin

[optional starting point:
how can I safely reconnect with the outdoors?
if I need to spend the day inside, how can I bring nature closer?
example: washing a window pane to allow clear, natural light.]

(xiii) **my response:**

(xiv)

is it a feeling of
disconnection
from the body and
mind?

or,
is it a feeling as if
both are breaking
down?

it's the pressing
harder

to get the
broken
body

to do what it needs
to ensure
today's survival.

but,
it's never given
enough nourishment
to be fully equipped
for tomorrow's.

[<u>optional starting point:</u>
how can I begin to strengthen, repair, and heal what needs to be
healed?]

(xiv) **my response:**

(xv)

I see you in your strength:
the quiet kind that
the breakneck-busy world misses,
the courage in getting up,
with iron determination
to continue
small steps forward.

[<u>optional starting point:</u>
asking again: what must I do in this moment to begin healing
what needs to be healed?
what must I do to move forward, even in small ways?]

(xv) **my response:**

part two: reflections (i - xv).

guidelines for reflections.

In this section, you will find a series of fifteen images including digital photographs and paintings. Each image is also paired with a question or series of related questions. Like the poetry fragments, allow yourself as much time as possible to pause and absorb the details of these images. Most of these artworks are abstracted to varying degrees, which allows rich ground for you to envision your own interpretation(s).

Visual art often has the ability to evoke responses beyond the logical, rational mind. As you navigate through this section, feel free to record any ideas, associations, feelings, and memories that may float to the surface. In time, you are welcome to bring in your analytical thought processes, especially if this is your natural operating mode. Yet, do not be afraid to record your very first thoughts. These may be fragmented and seemingly disconnected. They may even be syllables or sounds. For example, here's an initial response to the painting *Light Enters*:

"Filter, filtered, iridescent, abalone shell in dappled light, an hourglass, time, I need more rest, more unstructured time."

- If you feel inclined, take time to free-associate with each image. You can write your thoughts like the example above, or you can make a voice recording. Like with section one's poetry fragments, you have permission to write, paint, draw, collage, sing, dance, or whatever form(s) of creative expression you wish to try. Choose the method and medium that is the best fit for you in the moment.

- When you are ready to sift through the corresponding questions, you can continue the stream of consciousness approach. This may be what works best for you, especially if your energy levels are currently low. Otherwise, you may wish to spend extra time crafting your responses, allowing time for deep thought and answering each question as a journal entry.

- I strongly encourage you to compose your own guidelines.

- More than anything, I hope you will look upon each question and image as an opportunity to rest on the page.

Use the space below to list your unique ideas and approaches:

(i) **beauty.**

Light Enters, acrylic and mixed media on wood panel, 48 x 36 inches, 2018.

(i)

beauty.

What was something beautiful you recently encountered? There is beauty in traditional senses such as a bouquet of fragrant roses. There is bittersweet beauty in fall leaves' transition from green to gold and crimson, blanketing the ground before the first frost. And yet beauty is also found in the unexpected, such as a cloud that decides to stand alone in a monochrome of sky. When considering beauty, allow your definition to become more than what it was...

(i) **my response:**

(ii) **light.**

In Transit: View from Airplane Window (I), digital photo, dimensions variable, 2017.

(ii)

light.

When you think of light, what do you think of first? Light as in light from the sun? The experience of illumination, whether natural or artificial? Or, do you imagine light as in weight? This does not have to reference physical weight, rather it can be the feeling of lightness as an emotional weight is lifted from your shoulders.

(ii) **my response:**

(iii) **refashioning success.**

Suspension, layered digital photos, dimensions variable, 2021.

(iii)

refashioning success.

How can I refashion my ideas of success to continue moving forward, even in moments where little seems to be working in my favor? Courage is not only innate but can be practiced and grown. What are some ways I can refresh and renew myself to build my courage?

(iii) **my response:**

(iv) **space.**

Revisiting Edo, digital photo, dimensions variable, 2017.

(iv)

space.

If I were to craft a custom space for myself right now, what would I require? In this case, the idea of 'space' can be a physical place such as a home or geographic location but does not have be. Consider mental and emotional spaces, as well as making spaces for pause, spaces of silence.

(iv) **my response:**

(v) **movement.**

Without a Trace, layered digital photos, dimensions variable, 2011.

(v)

movement.

So much can be communicated through human gestures. If I take stock of my body right now, what is my posture, my breathing, the motions (or stillness) I am experiencing with my limbs? Am I energized by full-body movement, dance, running, and similar? Or, am I more drawn to small motions?

(v) **my response:**

(vi) **through a prism.**

Still, Motion, layered digital photos, dimensions variable, 2021.

(vi)

through a prism.

Consider the idea of experiencing the world by looking through a prism. On one hand, you may feel a sense of being fragmented, the view around you broken into endless shards like fractured glass. On the other hand, you may feel a sense of possibility with so many ways to look, to interpret. Can you think of and name one area in your life that may change dramatically if you shifted your vantage point?

(vi) **my response**:

(vii) **uncertainty...**
May Snowfall, digital photo, dimensions variable, 2019.

(vii)

uncertainty...

When presented with ambiguity, what is your response? With the image on the previous page, focus on your immediate emotional responses, sensations, feelings, and associations. Allow your intuition to take the primary role rather than logic. Do you feel nervous when guidelines are not set in advance, or do you relish the freedom? Or, do you fall somewhere in between?

There are countless answers, none of them wrong.

(vii) **my response:**

(viii) **daydream.**

Untitled, acrylic and mixed media on canvas, 12 x 9 inches, 2015.

(viii)

daydream.

Allow yourself a few moments in daydream. If your life is hectic, and there's little time to pause and imagine, this process may feel difficult or even painful at first. Even if you can only keep your mind focused on daydreaming for thirty seconds (or less), grant yourself that time. We are often trained to see our lives and the world in terms of limitations. What happens if we spend more time envisioning possibilities?

(viii) **my response:**

(ix) **setting.**
Mirrored Horizon, New Mexico, digital photo, dimensions variable, 2018.

(ix)

setting.

How do you interpret the phrase 'poetry of place?' What are the most distinguishing features of your current environment? You can interpret 'environment' as domestic spaces and elements of the landscapes that surround you (example, foothills and snow-capped mountains). Or, your current setting may be more connected to interior emotions and thoughts. How do you fit into (or contrast with) you present settings — physically, psychologically, emotionally, spiritually?

(ix) **my response:**

(x) **fragmented self.**

Fragmented Self, layered digital photos, dimensions variable, 2021.

(x)

fragmented self.

When we experience stress and pressure – whether this is sudden stress *(for example, the surprise loss of a family member)*, or prolonged pressure *(such as enduring and surviving a toxic work environment for months or even years)*, a side effect effect can manifest as a fragmented sense of self. We feel like we are choking in a fog, emotions are frozen, and we begin to question our thoughts and perceptions.

In what ways are you feeling fragmented or diffused? If you imagine yourself as fabric scraps of a quilt or worn threads in a woven tapestry, how might you begin stitching yourself back together...one tiny piece at a time?

(x) **my response:**

(xi) **stillness.**

In Transit: View from Airplane Window (II), digital photo, dimensions variable, 2017.

(xi)

stillness.

Stillness and silence are difficult to cultivate in our current era. This goes beyond the overwhelm of life's demands, information overload, and endless distractions. Deep down, we often have an unspoken fear of sitting along with our thoughts — what will emerge? Will I truly like the person I am if I take a close, uninterrupted look?

What comes up for you now, as you allow yourself a few moments of quiet?

(xi) **my response:**

(xii) **acceptance.**

Untitled, layered digital photos, dimensions variable, 2021.

(xii)

acceptance.

Here are some ways to look at acceptance: I accept things (*or a certain thing*) as is at this moment. I can be grateful for 'what is' right now, even if what is is not ideal. I can decide if I need or want to take steps to facilitate change. These steps can happen today or in the near future.

Can you pinpoint something you can sincerely accept in this very moment? Right now, can you name something you can both accept and be grateful for? What about an aspect of yourself that you accept and love?

(xii) **my response:**

(xiii) **innovation.**
Cycles, layered digital photos, dimensions variable, 2021.

(xiii)

innovation.

An expanded, richer, and more creative existence requires the willingness to innovate. Innovation can take the form of world-changing inventions, and innovation can also happen in the quiet of everyday life. What is something you do on a daily basis in the same or almost the same way? How can you begin to shift that habit or action? A simple example is eating your breakfast at a different seat at the table.

When you open yourself up to innovation, you often find small but powerful adjustments taking place in your life and work.

(xiii) **my response:**

(xiv) **preserve hope.**
HOPE, original poetry and paper collage on paper, 24 x 16 inches, 2020.

(xiv)

preserve hope.

Vincent van Gogh once described how the change of seasons helped him cling to hope in wider matters of life. In certain climates, wintertime brings frozen trees and plants, as well as darkness and seasons of hibernation. In time, this shifts. The ground thaws, trees begin to grow new leaves, and flowers blossom into a spray of pastel colors.

If you were to label your life in terms of seasons, which currently fits? You can think of this as winter, spring, summer, autumn. You can also think of this as initial planting, a growing season, harvest time, followed by a dormant season. What is a hope you have for your current season? If you find yourself in a difficult period, how might you cultivate hope for an eventual change in seasons?

(xiv) **my response:**

(xv) **mending.**

Fading Progression, ink, wax, and wool on kozo paper, 9.75 x 8.5 inches, 2014.

(xv)

mending.

There are moments or even periods in our lives where we may feel fragmented and fractured, like spiderweb cracks radiating through glass. You may feel this way if you have spent significant time becoming depleted, spread thinly across too many commitments, or managing chronic stress.

Consider this example: a ceramic bowl slips from a countertop and cracks into a half dozen pieces. Do you throw the bowl away, or do you try to mend the shards back into a whole?

In Japan, there's a concept called *kintsugi*, where pieces of broken pottery are mended with powdered precious metals such as gold or platinum. Kintsugi breathes life into what was once broken, highlighting the newfound strength, uniqueness, and beauty of each repaired piece.

How might you go about mending areas of your life?

What role can your creative work play in this process?

(xv) **my response:**

part three:
open space.

guidelines for open space.

This last section is for you to use entirely as you need and wish.

If you cannot think of where to begin, you can...

- Set aside pages to document the most memorable events of your day.
- Keep a record of how your creative work is progressing.
- Record new ideas and unexpected discoveries.
- Map out a plan to prioritize and implement daily rest and quiet. Make time to check in each evening.
- Free write until you cannot think of anything else to say and your mind feels clearer and calmer.
- Compose your own poetry. A simple way to begin is with a biography poem that highlights (1) words to describe you, (2) cherished relationships, (3) what you love, (4) vivid memories, (5) powerful fears, (6) your accomplishments, (7) dreams, and (8) your place of origin.

Here is an abbreviated example:

Miss Amelia,
a flurry of endless motion,
daughter of Byron and sister of Brendan,
lover of buttered noodles and Sunday stroller rides,
who fears running out of gumdrops and chocolate cookies,
performer of daredevil backbends and somersaults,
the only Californian born in our family,
Miss Amelia.

- Or, try something else entirely. Allow yourself space to reflect, dream, stretch, move, and imagine as much as you can...as much as you are ready.

open space:

(vi)

conclusion.

Dear reader, as you finish this book, I would like to leave you with one final thought:

If your art or creative practice needs to be therapeutic at this time in your life, *then let it be.*

As of autumn 2021, I still find myself filling journals, notebooks, and sketchbooks with a voracious appetite.

Yet, most of this is not writing as high art. It does not have to be.

If you were to crack open one of these books, you would find everything from anxieties about the state of the world to scribbled checklists of daily to-dos. Consistent writing, journaling, and creative making allow me to spill stream-of-consciousness thoughts, fears, and emotions onto paper. It also helps me cope with day-to-day life, keep exhaustion at bay, track small victories, and remind me of all that is going well so that I take time to be grateful.

In this flurry of ink-fueled chaos, I'll return at a later time to reread. Dear reader, I encourage you to do the same. This is when the discoveries happen, when we begin to uncover the small, golden kernels of ideas and insights. These will eventually become seedlings for poems, short stories, drawings, paintings, personal essays, and more.

If your art has to be *(...you fill in the blank...)* for a while, then let it be. If you have to temporarily press pause on your creative work to regain energy, please do so. Just make sure to come back to the work when and in all ways that you can. It may not seem productive now, but you will begin building that critical foundation for future projects – the kinds of projects that move you into the art you were meant to bring into the world.

With kindness and sincerity,
Erin

(vii)

acknowledgements.

Writing **(quiet, space).** has been one small step on the path of a longer – perhaps lifelong – journey. I could not have completed this book without my incredible traveling companions. I offer sincere gratitude to:

My husband, for seeing the gifts I can offer to the world, even when I cannot see them – and for encouraging me to share them.

My beautiful, spirited children. Everyday, you teach me that perceiving the world differently is not something to be ashamed of. It's a gift.

My mother and father, for providing their love and support on this career path.

All of my students of the past and present. You have each given me countless gifts in life lessons and creative inspiration.

Tracie, for always providing excellent feedback on how to make the writing better.

Kayla and Woz, for offering just the right kind of encouragement when the project became overwhelming.

Alex and Lindsey, for creating empowering opportunities for writers of all levels and backgrounds, and always in a spirit of generosity.

For Claire. Through nothing short of divine providence, you sent an encouraging note at just the right moment. Also, thank you for your beautiful sculpture that was the subject of the *innovation* photo.

Everyone who has encouraged me, whether consciously or accidentally, to pursue writing with greater dedication and confidence.

All others I have forgotten to mention by name who played roles in the art and writing tucked away in these pages.

All readers, for devoting their time to working through this book. May you find abundant benefits through rest and renewed creative practice.

(viii)

about the author.

Erin Schalk is a visual artist, writer, and educator who lives in the greater Los Angeles area. She graduated with her MFA in Studio from the School of the Art Institute of Chicago in 2017, and she has exhibited her art throughout the United States, as well as in the United Kingdom and Japan. In 2021, she was named the Muckenthaler Cultural Center's Artist in Residence – the third artist to receive this honor.

Both her poetry and visual art have been published in a variety of journals. Highlights include *The MacGuffin*, *The Woven Tale Press*, *Parentheses International Literary Journal*, *Willawaw Journal*, and others. Today, Schalk also is a guest poetry and visual art reviewer and interviewer for *Aji Magazine.*

In 2011, Schalk's career as an educator began overseas in Okinawa, Japan where she taught visual art and English as a Foreign Language (EFL). Since 2016, she has focused on teaching adults in non-profit and higher education settings. She also develops accessibility-driven art museum exhibitions, gallery spaces, and educational programs for individuals with visual impairments and on the autism spectrum.

Schalk also holds a BFA in Studio Art from the University of Oklahoma, a BA in East Asian Studies from the University of Maryland Asia, and an MA in Art from the University of Dallas.

She is the founder of *Bridging Art* (**www.bridgingart.com**) where she provides mentorship programs and workshops to emerging visual artists and writers of diverse ages and backgrounds, living across the globe. In addition, Schalk's professional artist website may be accessed at **www.erinschalk.com**.

(i x)

(quiet, space).

a quiet space for recovery, of unknotting in mind, body, and heart...

a space for being 'unproductive,' which is really productive –

a place for listening to the still, small voice.

www.ingramcontent.com/pod-product-compliance
Lightning Source LLC
Chambersburg PA
CBHW051109050726
47592CB00002B/736

* 9 7 8 0 5 7 8 3 1 1 1 0 4 *